BE CALM
SELF CARE GUIDE

FOR TEENS

IT'S TIME TO START LOVING YOU! TIPS, EXERCISES AND FUN FACTS TO GUIDE YOU THROUGH SELF CARE!

A MUST READ BOOK FOR ANY TEEN!

BY KATIE SMILE

© Copyright -Katie Smile 2021 - All rights reserved.

The content contained within this book may not be reproduced, duplicated or transmitted without direct written permission from the author or the publisher.

Under no circumstances will any blame or legal responsibility be held against the publisher, or author, for any damages, reparation, or monetary loss due to the information contained within this book. Either directly or indirectly. You are responsible for your own choices, actions, and results.

Legal Notice:

This book is copyright protected. This book is only for personal use. You cannot amend, distribute, sell, use, quote or paraphrase any part, or the content within this book, without the consent of the author or publisher.

Disclaimer Notice:

Please note the information contained within this document is for educational and entertainment purposes only. All effort has been executed to present accurate, up to date, and reliable, complete information. No warranties of any kind are declared or implied. Readers acknowledge that the author is not engaging in the rendering of legal, financial, medical or professional advice. The content within this book has been derived from various sources.

Please consult a licensed professional before attempting any techniques outlined in this book.

By reading this document, the reader agrees that under no circumstances is the author responsible for any losses, direct or indirect, which are incurred as a result of the use of the information contained within this document, including, but not limited to, — errors, omissions, or inaccuracies.

Introduction

Being a teenager is a whole lot of work. Sometimes, nobody understands you. Sometimes, it's like the entire world is against you. Trust me. I know how that feels. I've been there. It's like you're stuck in between. You're not an adult, and you're not a child. Your responsibilities become conflicting; you may not know what to do and when to do it.

This book, 'Be Calm: Self-Care Guide for Teens,' is a guide for teenagers, and it is packed with a lot of life hacks for you. It provides a breakdown of every aspect of self-care and the importance of prioritizing **you**!

When you're a teen, you have an excellent opportunity to start phasing good habits into your life. Yet, most of the time, stress from everyday ordeals can cause many to give up and settle for less. You deserve better than this! As you delve deeper into your enlightening journey, you will learn the various types of self-care and what works for you as an individual. Everyone is different, so naturally, our relaxation practices will also be unique. Just like, everyone's problems require their own solutions. But this book can give you the foundations of how to look after yourself so that you can find your personal path. Discover a brighter version of yourself, decide your own goals, and learn how to apply peace into your school and work life.

'Be Calm: Self-Care Guide for Teens' is a teenage shortcut to everything you need to know about self-care. The chapters are short and concise. This is so that you don't miss each chapter's point in the sea of many words. At the end of every chapter, there are fun exercises for you to participate in and more activities throughout the book! Let's get started and take your first step to a healthier you!

So, Why Should I *Care* About Self-Care?

It's simple: you NEED it!

First, what exactly is self-care?

Don't worry; I don't intend to bore you with something straight out of a textbook. You already had enough of that in school anyway. Now, hear me out. Self-care has nothing to do with being selfish or self-indulgent wherever you heard that from; quickly disregard it right here and now.

Self-care is all about looking after you. What about others? You might ask. I mean, when you are focused on yourself, you tend to disregard every other person, right? Your mom or dad? Well, no. If you can't be there for yourself, you are not mentally and physically capable of being there for others. It is that straightforward. It starts with you, and that is where self-care comes in. Prioritizing your health both physically and mentally and other aspects of self-care don't just make you capable of supporting friends and family. It also helps you cope with everything and anything happening around you.

Right now, just like any other teen, I'm sure you have a lot happening in your life, and more than ever, you need to know how to practice self-care to deal with them all. It starts today. Self-care demands that you check with yourself to know how you are doing and what your body needs.

#4 Types of Self-care

Yes, there are different types of self-care – specifically four types. Let's see what each has to offer.

Physical self-care: This covers everything that has to do with the physical part of you. Physical self-care practices range from prioritizing nutrition to exercise. Hold on; wondering how prioritizing nutrition and exercising are self-care practices? I mean, both you have cut out fizzy drinks, junks, and sweat out on the floor of your bedroom. They are self-care practices as nutrition and exercises ensure you get to visit the hospital less and overall be healthy. There, you are looking after yourself. What I am trying to say here is that physical self-care focuses on our physical well-being. You will learn more about physical self-care in one of the subsequent chapters.

Emotional self-care: So, you know we have physical health and mental health. Emotional self-care practices cater to our mental health. Emotions are complicated. As a teenager, it doesn't give you a break as you will experience so many new feelings. Talk about falling in love, breaking up, having a fight with your BFF, seeing your parents argue, and, in some cases, seeing your parents go their separate ways. All of these and more can be very difficult to handle. It's not like seeing our parents get divorced as a teenager is very different from when you are older. But certain factors stand out. You are younger;

you are most likely dependent on both; you live with them. So, these factors make it complicated to deal with the emotions that arise.

Hence, the need for self-care. No, self-care practices such as saying "no," managing stress, learning forgiveness, kindness, and emotional maturity won't make the pain go away or make everything make sense. However, it will help you handle your emotions better before it grows into something worse. Talk about depression, eating disorders, and anxiety - three common mental illnesses in teens.

Social self-care: This is closely related to emotional self-care. Let's just say they complement each other. Now, social self-care focuses on your relationships with people. You learn how to communicate. That's right! Proper communication goes beyond saying something. Communication involves you speaking, and somebody actually listens to what you have to say. With social self-care, you get to foster habits that help you better deal with people. As a teenager, this is something you will need. Yes, in high school, you interacted with loads of individuals. These guys are a tenth of whom you will have to associate with as you grow older. Don't let that scare you. As you grow older, it gets easier.

Spiritual self-care: practices spending time in nature, kindness, and meditating to help deal with the non-physical part of you; your soul or spirit. I will call it your mind instead. That part of you that exists, but no one sees, but you feel it.

It is this simple, as a teenager, you need to practice self-care to look after the physical, emotional, spiritual you and your relationship with others. That's it. No doubt, everyone needs self-care. Too much is happening in your life, and too little action is taken to prioritize your wellbeing. With self-care, you can have a perfect grip of your adult years. Without it, it could leave you having to deal with situations unprepared. Practicing self-care helps you understand this situation when they happen. You are not left hanging dry, and what more, you have more control over the spiritual, physical, and emotional parts of you. It's all about feeling great inside and out!

Prioritizing Self Care:
Day and Night Routine!

TAKING CARE OF ONE SELF IS SUCH A BIG DEAL THESE DAYS; MOST PEOPLE HAVE SELF-CARE ROUTINES, SKIN-CARE ROUTINES, AND DIET PLANS. MOST IMPORTANTLY EVERYONE NEEDS TO HAVE A DAY AND NIGHT ROUTINE! HERE IS ONE TO START WITH.

MORNING ROUTINE

1. WAKE UP!
2. Stretch your body!
3. NO PHONE
4. Wash your face
5. Brush your teeth.
6. Get dressed
7. Have breakfast
8. Start your day with a smile

NIGHT ROUTINE

1. Wash your face
2. Apply moisturizer
3. Brush your teeth
4. Brush your hair
5. Prepare your outfit
6. Organize your backpack
7. Create your to-do list for the next day
8. Relax with a screen-free activity

Say No to Junk food - NUTRITION is Life!

As a teen, I'm sure you hear all the time how important it is for you to eat well and to be healthy. The focus isn't on your body size but on the type of food that you eat. The best way to maintain good nutrition is by eating foods rich in fruits, nuts, whole grains, beans, eggs, lean meats, and fish. Eating such foods helps to lower the risks of obesity. It also supports bone growth and hormonal changes. You don't want to be left behind when your peers are wearing bras and developing deep voices, do you? Oh, eating good food would also reflect on your skin. As you grow, there is a need to increase nutrients like protein and iron and in calories. Eating fruit every day is a sure way to boost your health and general well-being. And about how much you should eat, that varies. The amount of food you eat should depend on your needs. Just make sure you aren't eating too much or too little.

The table below demonstrates just some of the benefits of eating particular fruit.:

Pineapples	Apples
Rich in potassium, calcium, vitamin C, beta carotene, thiamin, B6, as well as soluble and insoluble fiber.	Helps improve digestion, prevention of stomach disorders, gallstones, constipation, liver disorders.
Lemons	**Oranges**
Has nutritional elements like vitamin C, vitamin B6, vitamin A, vitamin E, folate, niacin thiamin, and riboflavin.	Boosts immune system function, reduce signs of aging, protect against cancer, and boost cellular repair.

Of course, in addition, drink a lot of water to stay hydrated. Sodas may be tasty, and all but they are full of empty calories. Try skipping soda for a day or two and drink water instead. You'll be doing yourself a big favor because, as a teen, water keeps spots away from your skin. It makes you look fresh and beautiful

#5 Food habits you should adopt:
1. Always eat breakfast
2. Drink lots of water and stay hydrated
3. Eat lots of fruit and veg
4. Reduce salt intake
5. Eat more fish

FUN FACTS: *Eating nutritious food will contribute to healthier, brighter skin. Water is the secret ingredient to spot-free skin.*

Practice Exercise:
1. Create a healthy food timetable for yourself.
2. Go on a one-week, no soda/ sugar drinks challenge.

Exercise is the way to go; Sweat it Out!

Everyone's paying regular visits to the gym these days because they want a great body. That's awesome. But do you know exercising goes beyond that? Exercising boosts your energy level. It helps to release tension and to manage stress. It is an essential part of keeping you healthy. And don't be one of those who say they'll start exercising when they get older. If you can't do push-ups now, what's the probability you'll be able to do it five years from now?

Start by establishing a daily routine. You can plan it out with your family or your friends. It'll be nice if you have someone to work out with. Exercising for 30 minutes per day would help to maintain good health and physical fitness.

Some of the exercises you could do (probably at home) are dancing, brisk walking, climbing stairs, running, swimming, hiking, soccer, jumping rope, and roller skating.

Hare a few exercises you can do anywhere:

STRETCHES

Before you start your day or even before any exercise you need to stretch your body. The picture above illustrates a few stretch poses for you to try.

SQUATES

LET'S GET FIT!

Stand as straight as you can, with your hands stretched in front of you. The fingers should be pointed forward. Keep your legs apart to shoulder length. Push your upper body down from the hips, and go down as you bend your knees. Be careful so that your knees do not cross your feet, but your lower body should bend as low as possible, meanwhile bending down you should still be able to see your feet. Slowly, push yourself back to the standing position. Do not bend your back or the hands at any given time.

LUNGES

Stand straight with your hands on your hips and keep your back straight. Your feet should be at least one foot wide apart, and your shoulders should be pointed straight. Keep your focus forward. Take a big step with your right leg by lowering your hips and bending your right knee and the left knee to a 90-degree angle. The right knee should be right above the right foot, and the left knee (at the back) should not be touching the ground. Stay in the position for five seconds and come back to the starting position. Repeat this for a at least 10 times.

EXERCISE - TRACKER

	MON	TUES	WED	THU	FRI
Stretching for 15 mins	○	○	○	○	○
15 Lunges	○	○	○	○	○
20 or more Squats	○	○	○	○	○
Running for 30 mins	○	○	○	○	○
50 or more sit ups	○	○	○	○	○

TICK ALL COMPLETED CIRCLES, USE PENCIL.

Feeling tired? Quit Chatting and Go to Bed!

TEEN'S WORSE SELF CARE HABIT IS BED ROUTINE!

In this age where every teenager owns a smartphone, teenagers no longer get enough sleep. Research shows that as a teen, you need at least 8 hours of sleep every night. And some of you are barely even getting five! Sleep deprivation can have harmful effects on you, resulting in concentration difficulties, truancy, lack of enthusiasm, memory impairment, and clumsiness and you don't want that do you?

Learn to put your phone away when it's bedtime. Set yourself a time before bed e.g. 9pm where you will have NO screen-time.. Literally not even a peek! The best thing to do if you're a tough sleeper is to read a book or listen to relaxing music.

Maintain this schedule for at least a month and you will notice a drastic change in your quality of sleep and your concentration levels. As a result you will have a better attitude and will be more enthusiastic to facing your day, regardless if you are a morning person or not.

FUN FACTS: Did you know there is an 80% chance for someone to appear in your dreams because they miss you!

Self- Care Check: Practice Exercise

1. Create a relaxing bedtime routine for yourself.
2. Create a healthy food timetable for yourself.
3. Go on a one-week, no soda/ sugar drinks challenge.
4. Create a 30-minute exercise routine for yourself, which you would do every day.
5. Create a bedtime routine for yourself. This should include the time you go to bed every day, have a bath or drink before bed, or meditating.

Fix a time for keeping your phone away, or your computer and TV each day and ask your mum (or any other person) to help keep you in check.

Turn to the next page for a Self-care checklist. Tick of the boxes of activities you do to look after yourself and prioritize your self being. If you find yourself to have ticked most of the boxes, well done you are clearly taking the steps to care for yourself.

self-care check-in

CHECK THE BOXES OF THE ACTIVITIES YOU DO TO TAKE CARE OF YOURSELF.

- [ ] EAT THREE MAIN MEALS
- [ ] GO ON A 24-HOUR SOCIAL MEDIA DETOX
- [ ] FIND A QUIET SPOT TO MEDITATE
- [ ] LIGHT AN AROMATIC CANDLE
- [ ] DO A GRATITUDE LIST
- [ ] PRACTICE DEEP BREATHING
- [ ] LISTEN TO NEW GENRE OF MUSIC
- [ ] EXERCISE
- [ ] CATCH UP WITH A FRIEND
- [ ] VISIT A FAMILY MEMBER
- [ ] SPEND TIME OUTDOORS
- [ ] HAVE A MINI PAMPER SESH
- [ ] READ A BOOK
- [ ] TRY SOMETHING NEW

Stabilizing those Crazy Hormones for Mental Health!

Mental health is predominant with teens and often hostile. The rampant hormones in teens make it challenging to take the right approach and deal with the impending mental health. So, in other words, puberty causes you to be stressed out, which could, if not cared for, elevate into mental health problems such as depression and anxiety. This is because puberty brings a certain level of unstable behavior, attitudes, thoughts, and especially mood swings which, if not handled properly, could get out of control, and cause adverse effects on your mental health. During adolescence, you are going through phases of a lot of crazy emotions due to your hormone levels. But that's okay, everyone goes through it. As you read on you will learn many tips and techniques to handle your negative thoughts, learn to maintain calm and have a positive mindset.

So, what do you need to do?

It is that simple, practice emotional self-care habits. Self-care habits put you above these fluctuating hormones like estrogen, testosterone, and progesterone in such a way that you effectively deal with your psychological self. Self-care teaches you to prioritize your needs first before you leave yourself neglected.

FUN FACTS: Did you know teens are more likely to be easily obsessed and addicted to things than any other age group because of their teen's brain's puberty development.

Self-care techniques to Stabilize Hormones

Let's look at few self-care techniques that help with hormonal balance.

Alternate Nostril Breathing

Basically, this is simply a unique breathing exercise. If you are into yoga, you would already be familiar with nostril breathing. What makes this form of breathing unique is that you don't breathe through both of your nostrils at a go but one after the other. That covers it.

Practicing alternative nostril breathing will help you release stress and especially balance both hemispheres of your brain. I mean, your brain controls those hormones, right? Balance it, and you automatically balance your hormones. Alternate nostril breathing is easy to do, doesn't require any special technique or gear in particular. All you need is a space to practice without yelling from either your parents or your siblings - if you have any.

Disconnect from technology. What if I told you that your mobile phone, PC contribute to stress? Somehow, I think you already know this. Emails, text messages, social media notifications, each time your phone or PC buzzes for any of these, you rattle your stability. OK, I know that sounds extreme, but hear me out. When you receive a notification, you are compelled to attend to it. Now see, it interrupts whatever you are doing, and it automatically becomes a distraction. I know you have group projects that you need to see to by answering those emails and text messages. And no, you can't just live without your electronics because we are not in 1200; so yeah, you will need your electronics. However, why don't you put a latch on it instead? I mean, you could do without your mobile or PC one day a week, right just for the sake of your wellbeing?

Practice Exercises

1. Practice Alternate Nostril Breathing for 5 minutes first thing in the morning. Increase to 10 minutes after the second week and 15 minutes after the first month. Stick with 15 minutes as long as you want.

2. Disconnect one day a week. Start with Saturday, the first week. Extend to Saturday and Sunday after the first month of successfully disconnecting your phone every Saturday

Meditation: Stress Relief Poses

Meditation can take your stress away and allow you to sustain a tranquil mind. It teaches you how to detach and eliminate any negative thoughts by finding your inner calmness.

Lotus

Sit with your back straight and your legs folded, take a deep breath and find your inner peace. Try and do this pose for 2 minutes

Corpse position:

This pose is to relax your whole body. Just lay flat on your back with your arms rested on the floor, palms facing upwards. Relax your body and allow your feet to lay outwards. Do this pose for 5 minutes.

Turn to the next page for 15 stress relief poses to help you relax and destress from a hard day!

15 Yoga poses for Stress Relief

Easy poses   Seated *twist*   Cow *face*   Cobbler *pose*

One legged *downward facing dog*   Triangel *forward*   Warrior *II poses*   Shoulderstand

Seated *forward bend*   Extended *puppy*   Downward *facing dog*

Leg up   Hight *lunge*   Forward *fold*   Bridge *poses*

Keeping your Friends Close and your Family Closer

How much time did you spend with your family as a teenager? Do you feel like family isn't vital and only your friends' matter? Or do you feel like both your family and friends aren't important and social media is your only priority? Your answers to these questions are important because whether you like it or not, family time is an essential factor in your total well-being.

I know it's hard to get the whole family to spend time together, especially if you're a teenager and you have younger siblings, and then there are your parents. What could you guys possibly be talking about? Well, there are a lot of ways you can make family time work out.

One way is by showing interest in all your family members' lives. If you don't care about your younger sister, how's she going to care about you? Ask her about her homework and her classmates. Ask your dad about work. Show interest in what's going on in their lives, and they'll do the same to you.

When your mum or dad is trying their best to plan fun family activities, please don't ruin it. Join them to get ice cream. Bake with them in the kitchen. Watch movies with them on Sunday night. Go on field trips with them. Research has shown that six hours a week of family time can make a huge difference in a teenager's wellbeing.

Ever Tried Camping/Glamping?

You should try camping. It helps you reconnect with people and connect with nature. It allows you to unplug for a while. And oh, let's not forget the fresh air, the beautiful scents of the outdoors. Outdoors is key to healthy well-being. It's essential to get some sunlight. It's known to increase your happiness and contributes to a healthy skin glow.

Bring those friends along! Taking your friends to camp with you is like killing two birds with one stone. You get to go camping, and you get to bring the social scenes with you! Instead of texting your best friends about what you're doing, they get to experience it with you!

One more thing that's going to make camping fun is being a part of the planning. Join your parents in making plans. Help them choose a destination or a campground or the meals. This way, you can even sneak in some of your favorite activities you'd love to do!

Self Care: Outdoors Activity Rule 101

Leave the electronics at home! Whether it's camping or another fun activity, it is a way to bond and maybe reconnect with friends and family. You cannot do that if you're texting all the while, you're there. The only way to fully enjoy your outing experience is to participate 100% and do what everyone else is doing. How can you ever meet someone new or have a connection when you are constantly distracted by technology. Your computers, smartphones, video games, and iPods should be left at home or in the car.

Choose your priorities wisely!

Do you relate well with the people around you, or do you only have a relationship with your smartphone? Do not let social media fool or hypnotize you. You need people. You need to have people around. Ever heard the saying, "Man is not an island"? It's impossible to survive alone because humans are made to depend on each other to survive. You need people to support you, motivate you, and show you love. You need to spend time with friends and family. Do not let your life revolve around the Internet. There's more around you than you can see. The only way to find out what this "more" is, is by looking deeper. You need to take time off your computer or your phone and observe what's going on in reality. There are so many things to do with your family and friends, so many memories to make unless of course, you would rather watch someone else live their best life for you? No, thank you! Am I right?

FUN FACTS: *42% of teenagers can text even with their eyes closed! But when they receive messages from their parents, they tend to ignore them.*

Practice Exercise:

1. Plan a camping trip with your family.

2. Plan a camping trip with your friends.

3. Suggest to your family members that you guys bake a cake or cupcakes.

4. Join your family in the sitting room this weekend (especially if you usually don't)

9 DAYS CHALLENGE

CHALLENGE YOURSELF ON THIS SELF VALIDATION JOURNEY

Day 1	Day 2	Day 3
Write a letter to your future self	Set your weekly goals	Go for an evening stroll
Day 4	Day 5	Day 6
Watch your favorite series	Log out from your social media	Spend time with family and friends.
Day 7	Day 8	Day 9
Say positive words to yourself	Learn something new	Go for a full body care treatment

Growth Mindset: If You Think You Can, You Can!

What does it mean to have a growth mindset? Well, it is when a student understands that their abilities can be developed. Having a growth mindset is you believing that you can do better than you are doing now. It assumes that you can always catch up, improve, and even surpass the others. A teenager with a growth mindset believes that through dedication and hard work, they can achieve anything and can develop their basic abilities. This mindset is beneficial because it births this love for learning which is vital for great accomplishment.

For you to grow effectively, you need to believe that you can grow. It all starts with the mind. You can't pass your exams if you believe the subject is too complicated for you to pass. You can't master a skill if you think it's too difficult. Everything starts with the mind, and that is why, at all times, you need to feed your mind with healthy thoughts.

The question now is, what area of your life should you apply the growth mindset to? The answer is every area! In your education, personal life, or relationship, you should always have the attitude that you can do better. See in the picture below the different types of attitudes a growth mind portrays. You are young. You have the opportunity to learn new things every day, with every chance you get so let your mind grow!

Looking at the picture what side you would you be on?
GROWTH MINDSET OR FIXED MINDSET?

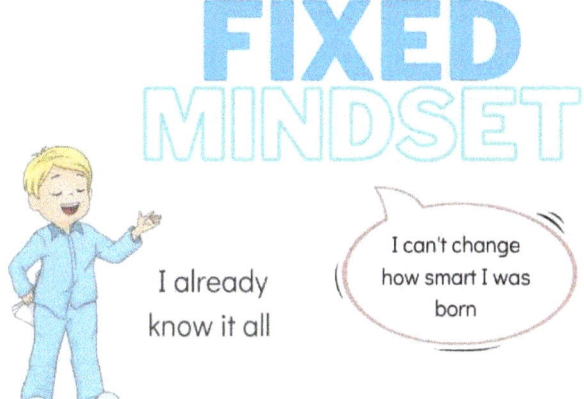

FIXED MINDSET

I already know it all

I can't change how smart I was born

I give up easily

I ignore useful feedback

I avoid things that require effort

Mistakes and failure are bad so I avoid them

I won't ever be good at this

I don't need to practice

GROWTH MINDSET:

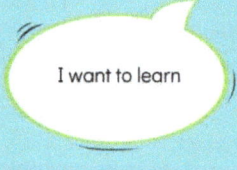

GROWTH

M — I learn from my mistakes

I — I can improve through hard work

N — I never give up

D — I am determined

S — Success comes from self-reflection

E — Effort will help me see improved results

T — I always try my best

Discovering a New Hobby makes Life so much more exciting!

Think of a hobby as anything you can do that's not compulsory and doesn't earn you money. Dancing isn't your hobby if your mum is constantly forcing you to go for dance lessons. A hobby is something you do because you want to do it. It's something you do outside of school hours. It's something you're happy doing. And you know what? Research shows that teenagers with hobbies are less likely to engage in high-risk behaviors. Teens without hobbies or who do not partake in extra-curricular activities are more likely to use drugs, smoke cigarettes, get arrested, and become teen parents in high school. When you have too much time on your hands, you may spend it doing something not that.

When you have hobbies, you have a chance to meet new people, discover your passion, manage time, build your self-esteem, learn the value of hard work, find out who you are, regulate your emotions and feel a sense of achievement. I mean what more could you want right? But if you struggle to motivate yourself in trying something new, I have created a calendar for you to help you take your first steps.

FUN FACTS: Did you know SINGING is known to reduce anxiety and depression!

7-Day Self-Care Routine

DAY 1

- Attempt a balanced diet - You can pretend it's junk food!
- Set a schedule for the week
- Exercise for one hour
- Create sleep routine
- Take a walk

DAY 2

- Attempt a balanced diet
- Start saving money
- Try out something new
- Meditate
- Watch Inspirational Youtube
- Take a stroll

DAY 3

- Attempt a balanced diet
- Meet up with a friends
- Have one hour for yourself
- Learn a skill
- Read a book
- Listen to podcast

DAY 4

- Attempt a balanced diet
- Practice cooking with family or friends
- Read your school books
- Attend group studies

DAY 5

- Attempt a balanced diet
- Treat yourself nice
- Pamper yourself
- Create a playlist for you!
- Full body work out

DAY 6 & 7

- Attempt a balanced diet
- Spend time with family
- Put your phone or computer away
- Watch television with family in the evening
- Cook with your family

MY WEEKLY SELF CARE ROUTINE

MONDAY **TUESDAY** **WEDNESDAY**

THURSDAY **FRIDAY** **SATURDAY**

SUNDAY

Self-Care: Managing your Money!

Don't spend it, save it! I can tell you now that is the best advice anyone can give you. The more money you save, the more money you will have in the long run. Yes, as a teen, I'm sure you think that is quite a challenging thing to do, especially when there are so many amazing things to spend the money on!

Well, here are your options. You can easily spend your money on items you don't need. But say you didn't. Say the next time your parents or relatives give you money, you store it and don't spend it. Forget it even exists. Then comes the next time and the next, and even any money you have spare can all be added to your money pot. Just imagine a year later how much money you will have if you just don't spend it on things you don't need? It's A LOT isn't it?. Rather than buying a small game, you will instead be able to buy the whole console yourself, probably with the game included. Well, that's a made-up scenario. However, the process of it is accurate. If you have even a small amount of money, you have a choice of spending it straight away on a small item that will give you slight satisfaction, or you can save it and buy something more significant and get much greater happiness.

Let's make some Money Exercise: Set yourself a goal of the amount you want to save and go for it! Save every penny cent spared! You will be shocked by the result.

HOW TO OPEN a BANK ACCOUNT

In order to save your money wisely, it will be ideal to open a bank account that will protect and store your money over a long period of time. Some banks offer interest on savings accounts which just basically means by having your money in the savings account, the bank will be adding a small percentage on top of your amount over a period of time as long as you keep the money in there. All you need to do is either go to the bank or access the online application form, which you will need to fill in to open a bank account. It's that simple! In the meantime, you can go to the next page and use the savings tracker.

GOAL:

SAVING:

DATE	AMOUNT

TOTAL:

How to apply Self Care at School or work

Time Management
Nothing is worse than waking up on the wrong foot in the morning and starting the day unprepared. It sets you up for an anxious day that could easily be avoided through preparation and time management. This is why a good sleep routine is needed to have a healthy balance. Not only does it support healthy brain development, but it also helps you organize and structure your everyday routine.

Here are few things you should consider before going to bed :

1. Is your bag packed and clothes ready for the next day?
2. Are your homework and assignments up to date?
3. Is your journey route planned (if needed)
4. Have you set your alarm?

Time management is crucial in order to be successful in life especially as you head towards adulthood. If you are late for school you might just get detention or a warning, but when you become an adult and if you're late for work, there will be high consequences, and you could lose your job. So as a teen, it is important to develop a habit of getting yourself into a good routine to make your life run as smoothly and stress-free as possible.

Set Boundaries

As a teen, it is also important to set boundaries as an essential aspect of self-care. It's okay to say NO if it means prioritizing your well-being. You are overwhelmed with assignment deadlines, exams and have high social needs, which all requires a lot of energy. So it is crucial to prioritize the important things in your life that contribute to the success of your well-being as opposed to the adverse effects caused by not having your priorities straight. You must outweigh the pros and cons and make the decision based on what will be the most beneficial outcome for you and your mental health. So if it means cancelling a party or friends gathering because you have an exam tomorrow that will, in the long run, it will be beneficial to your future, it's okay to say no! You are prioritizing your greater satisfaction of passing your exam and being successful in the future, over short-term gratification with small outcomes and rewards.

Everyone needs a Support system

Whether it is at school, at home, or even in life, it is essential to have someone to turn to. To share all your fears, worries, or even just to have someone to talk to. A support system is vital to a healthy state of mind, especially as a teen. Whether it's your best friend, relative, or even your teacher, unload yourself with any worries, share your thoughts. Trust me, you will feel so much better!

Here are few tips to help you if you feel overwhelmed at school:

1. Take a break and hydrate. Dehydration can negatively affect your mood.

2. Make a playlist of your favorite music. Create a few playlists of different styles of music.
   You will sometimes find listening to a different genre can change your mood.

3. Check yourself: if you feel you find yourself saying 'i can't do this or 'it's too much, that means you need to take a pause. This is where your support system comes in. It's a lot easier doing something together with some help from a friend or relative than having to do everything by yourself, including when you are feeling anxious and overwhelmed.

4. Move yourself to a more positive environment. If you find the people around you are affecting your mood negatively or making you feel uncomfortable, just remove yourself from the situation. You will find that quite often in life there

are some people who just take up all your energy and time and consume your life. This is where, as mentioned previously; you need to set boundaries. It's okay to say NO and remove yourself from the negativity.

5. Most importantly, take a breather. Learn to take some time for yourself and get all your thoughts together, whether it's excusing yourself to go to the toilet and have some privacy there or going outside for a few minutes just to be alone with you. This time is crucial as it allows you to listen to yourself, your needs, and what would make you happy? You then pull yourself and carry on!

Regardless of what techniques you use for self-care, it is important to prioritize yourself. Your well-being always comes first. In order to help someone else, you sometimes need to help yourself first. It is only through a healthy state of mind that you can reach your full potential and succeed in life. There are no limits. As long as you are looking after yourself, eating well, exercising, and most importantly, maintaining your happiness, you will glide through life and its stressors.

FUN FACTS: Did you know 70% of teens would avoid going to school because of how they looked. So if you ever felt this way you are definitely not alone!

Turn to the next page and write down your future goals; let your dreams run wild. Once you have written down your future goals, you are more likely to take more responsibility and aim towards them. Your whole life is ahead of you, with so many exciting milestones to look forward to. Let your imagination take you away to the future that will be your life. Chase your dreams, don't run from them regardless of how scary it may seem. As they say, 'nothing worth having comes easy.'

ME, MYSELF AND MY GOALS

THE JOB I HOPE TO HAVE ONE DAY:

A PLACE IN THE WORLD I WANT TO LIVE:

A PET I WANT TO HAVE:

A CRAFT I WANT TO LEARN SOON:

A SKILL I WANT TO MASTER:

MY DREAM HOUSE:

CONCLUSION

Your health, your relationships, and your mindset are important factors that you need to prioritize as a teenager to a healthy and happy life. In terms of your health, you need to eat the right meals at the right time and in the right proportion. Exercising is also vital. Try to incorporate it into your daily routine and stick to it.

Remember that exercising doesn't necessarily mean going to the gym. There are many exercises you can do at home, your room or outdoors. So no excuses! Being fit and healthy is crucial to maintaining a happy growth. And lastly, the most important aspect of your life is your sleep. Never estimate the power of a good sleeping pattern. They don't call it beauty sleep for no reason! Remember that you should have at least 8 hours of sleep a night as a teenager to be healthy.

In this book, we also discussed your relationship with friends and family. Family time is important whether you're six or sixteen years old. Try as much as possible to find time for your family. Go camping with them, watch television with them, cook with them, just spend time with them! Trust me when I say memories last a lifetime. The same goes for friendships, plan sleepovers with your friends, invite them to go camping with your family. Do not neglect them! Real life communication is so much more better and effective than via telephone or the net.

And lastly, we talked about finding new hobbies. There are about one thousand and one things you can do. Don't settle for one and give up hope when you don't do it well. Keep trying till you find something you are good at.

Eat good food, exercise regularly, sleep early, spend time with family and friends and always try new things! The secret to a happy life!

REFERENCES

D.M.L. (2021). *Physical and Hormonal Changes During Puberty Can Cause Depression.* Verywell Mind. https://www.verywellmind.com/depression-during-puberty-1067561

Germaine. (2021, February 4). *Self Care Routine for Hormones: Top Tips to Get Started.* Live Well Zone. https://livewellzone.com/create-self-care-routine-tips/

Lawler, M., & Laube, J. (2020, April 5). *What Is Self-Care and Why Is It Critical for Your Health? | Everyday Health.* EverydayHealth.Com. https://www.everydayhealth.com/self-care/

M.D. (2018b). *Is It a Mental Health Problem? Or Just Puberty? | NAMI: National Alliance on Mental Illness.* Alliance on Mental Health. https://www.nami.org/Blogs/NAMI-Blog/May-2018/Is-It-a-Mental-Health-Problem-Or-Just-Pubery

Monroe, J. (2020, June 3). *Teenage Hormones and...* Newport Academy. https://www.newportacademy.com/resources/empowering-teens/teenage-hormones-and-sexuality/

Developing a self-care plan. (2018). Teacher Wellbeing | ReachOut Schools. https://schools.au.reachout.com/articles/developing-a-self-care-plan

Self-care and teenagers - ReachOut Parents. (2018). Self Care for Teenagers. https://parents.au.reachout.com/skills-to-build/wellbeing/self-care-and-teenagers#

Gongala, S. (2015, July 22). *29 Impressive Workout For Teenage Girls.* MomJunction. https://www.momjunction.com/articles/workout-plans-for-your-teenage-girl_00364027/

10 Self-Care Tips for College Students. (2018). Make School. https://www.makeschool.com/blog/10-selfcare-tips-for-college-students

Weird but True: 7 Fun Facts about Teens. (2017, April 11). Kids Cell Phone Monitoring Issues | Pumpic Blog. https://pumpic.com/security/fun-facts-about-teenagers/

A. (2020, December 17). *Teenagers Psychological Facts- 33 Golden Facts about Teenagers.* A Treasure of General Knowledge. https://gkaim.com/psychological-facts-about-teenagers/

Mawunyo, J. Y., & Mawunyo, J. Y. (2020, October 16). *How To Develop and Maintain Healthy Eating Habits.*

WordInspired. https://dailywordinspired.com/health/how-to-develop-and-maintain-a-healthy-eating-habit/